WHAT PLANE IS THAT?

WHAT PLANE IS THAT?

Maurice Allward

OCTOPUS

First published 1979 by
Octopus Books Limited
59 Grosvenor Street
London W1

ISBN 0 7064 0982 5

Produced by Mandarin Publishers Limited
22a Westlands Road, Quarry Bay, Hong Kong

Printed in Singapore

CONTENTS

INTRODUCTION

The first flight in a powered aircraft was made by the Wright Brothers on 17 December 1903.

The next ten years saw aircraft develop slowly into machines often more fragile than the one the Wrights used, but easier to fly, generally more reliable and, because of their wheeled under-carriages, certainly easier to move around on the ground.

When World War I started in 1914, however, aircraft were still largely a novelty. Although some thought had been given to the possibility of using them for military purposes, the Armies involved had ideas for using aircraft only for reconnaissance and the Navies had vague ideas for patrol work. In the opening days of the war aircraft were unarmed, and if a pilot spotted an enemy, all he could do to frighten him was to make faces and shake his fists.

Four short years later, however, pilots in fast, heavily-armed fighter 'planes were shooting each other out of the sky; reconnaissance 'planes were reporting and photographing movements of armies on the ground and fleets at sea; bombers were dropping high-explosive and incendiary bombs on battlefields and on towns; the first dive bombers had been built to terrify infantrymen on the ground and to destroy concrete and steel forts; torpedo planes had scored their first victories against ships at sea; fragile seaplanes had largely given way to rugged carrier-based fighters and bombers; and big long-range flying-boats had been built for anti-submarine duties.

In Britain alone, the aircraft industry grew from a few small 'back-yard' garages into a vast complex of factories employing over a quarter-of-a-million people, and producing warplanes at the incredible rate of 30,000 a year.

Orville Wright, pilot of the Flyer in 1903, said sadly 'What a dream it was; what a nightmare it has become.'

From this nightmare have evolved the warplanes, the bombers and the fighters, described in this book. But from the same nightmare have evolved more pleasant types of aircraft, ranging from the giant civil airliners which can carry hundreds of passengers thousands of miles, to the small two, three and four-seat club aircraft used for afternoon joy rides in much the same way as people use cars.

Many of the famous aircraft (and some of those which are less well known but still interesting) both warplanes and civil types, are described and illustrated in this book. In many cases, then, this book will help you to answer the question 'What Plane Is That?' whenever anyone asks you.

RESEARCH AIRCRAFT

Right from the earliest days of flying, special research aircraft have been built to try out new ideas.

For example, the Wright Brothers flew full-size unmanned models and experimental gliders, during the development of their famous powered *Flyer* of 1903,

In the following years other pioneers designed aircraft with one, two, three or four wings, and with straight wings and curved wings, to try to find solutions which would make flying easier.

When it became apparent that the monoplane or biplane wing, together with a tailplane and fin and rudder, was the best general configuration, the research became more specialized. Different wing

sections were tried along with different motors.

In 1937, Britain invented the first really successful jet engine, the Whittle W1. This was flown in 1941 in an experimental aircraft, the Gloster Type E.28/39, before the revolutionary engine was used to power a new generation of super-fast fighters and bombers. A similar experimental jet aircraft, the He 178, was used by the Germans. This aircraft, in fact, flew nearly two years before the E.28/39. The first American jet research aircraft, the Bell XP-59A, flew in October 1942.

When aircraft began nudging the 'sound barrier', research aircraft were built to take aviation over this technological hurdle. Because they were fearful of the danger involved, Britain developed a

series of bomb-like models which were dropped from aircraft and their behaviour studied as they plummeted towards the ground.

America, however, built a full-size aircraft, the rocket-powered Bell X-1, which made the first manned supersonic (faster than the speed of sound) flights in October 1947. This pioneering research aircraft helped to give America a lead in the development of high-performance aircraft which she retains to this day. In the United States it lead, indirectly, to the North American X-15, one of the most remarkable research aircraft ever built. The X-15 was launched in the air from the wing of a specially adapted B-52 bomber, when its own rocket motor was switched on. Three X-15s were built and during their years of test flying, achieved a maximum speed of 7,254 kmph (4,534 mph). At the height they flew the air is so thin that the pilots were given special 'astronaut wings', signifying that they had virtually flown into space.

As most aircraft accidents occur during landing, one of the best ways to make flying safer would be to make landing easier. One way to do this is to enable aircraft to land more slowly, or, best of all, vertically. Helicopters have always had this capability, but it was not until the advent of the jet engine that it became practical for conventional fixed-wing aircraft.

As often happens, the first application of jet lift was seen in a military aircraft – Britain's Harrier.

This fighter has so many obvious advantages that it is not surprising that a large number of current research aircraft are attempts at applying the principle of jet lift to existing successful fixed-wing designs. Other research aircraft, such as those with tilting wings, or tilting rotors, are investigating new methods of achieving a short take-off or vertical take-off capability, and combining this with the ability to fly fast in level flight.

Some of these exciting research aircraft are described in the following pages, so that you will be able to tell 'What research aircraft that was.'

DASSAULT MIRAGE III-V

A fighter that can take-off and land vertically will often be able to fight when a conventional aircraft is out of action because of bomb-damaged runways. Because of this several designers have tried to add a vertical take-off capability to a successful conventionally-designed fighter.

One such VTOL (vertical take-off and land) research aircraft was this version of the very successful French Mirage fighter modified in the mid nineteen-sixties. On this aircraft vertical lift was obtained by eight Rolls-Royce RB 162 lift jets, mounted vertically in four pairs.

Development of this research aircraft was stopped after a series of accidents even though it had made many successful flights, and flown faster than the speed of sound. (*above*)

MARTIN X-24B

This unusual wingless research aircraft was built to help the development of manned aircraft able to operate in orbit as a spacecraft, fly in the Earth's atmosphere like aircraft and land at conventional airports.

It could not take-off by itself, but was launched in the air from beneath the wing of a Boeing B-52 'motherplane'. Once launched the pilot switched on a 3,300 kg (8,000 lb) thrust rocket motor, when a speed of 1,600 kmph (1,000 mph) could be reached at 18,290 m (60,000 ft). The lift was mainly generated by the specially-shaped 'lifting-body' fuselage.

Experience gained on the X-24B helped the development of the Space Shuttle described at the end of the section. (*right*)

10

NORTH AMERICAN XB-70 VALKYRIE

This snake-like aircraft was designed to be a long range bomber able to fly
to targets up to 6,400 kilometres (4,000 miles) away at a speed of 3,200 kmph
(2,000 mph). Through changes in policy, however, only two aircraft were
built and these were used for aerodynamic research. One of the aircraft was
lost when a Lockheed F104 escort collided with it at the end of a test flight.

The delta-winged XB-70 was designed to make use of 'compression lift' caused
by compressing the air flowing under the wing. At supersonic speed the air was
forced to pass under the wing between folded-down hinged wing tips and a huge
nacelle containing the six engines. At low speeds the wing tips were raised to their
normal position. (*above*)

LING-TEMCO-VOUGHT XC-142

Conventional fixed-wing aircraft can fly fast, but cannot land slowly. Helicopters can take-off and land vertically, but cannot fly as fast as fixed-wing aircraft.

Designers have tried out many novel schemes to try to produce an aeroplane that can fly fast but land slowly, but none of which have been completely successful. One fairly popular idea is to have a tilting wing, so that the engines can be pointed upwards for take-off and landing, and tilted down for normal cruising flight. The Ling-Temco-Vought XC-142 was one such tilt-wing aircraft. Although it flew quite successfully on tests, it was not put into production because of its complicated machinery. (*top*)

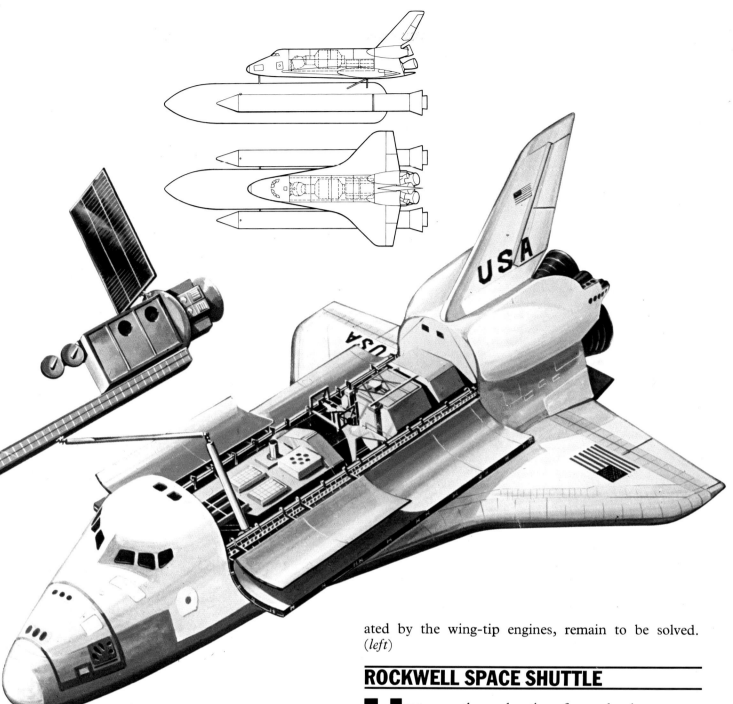

DORNIER Do-31

The Dornier Do-31 was an ambitious research aircraft, built in 1967, applying the principle of jet lift to a VTOL transport aircraft.

Most of the lift was provided by two banks of four Rolls-Royce RB 162 engines, mounted in pods at the wing tips and developing a total of 14,583 kg (35,000 lb) thrust. This was supplemented during take-off by the deflected, or 'vectored' thrust of two Bristol Siddeley Pegasus turbofans, which added another 9,583 kg (23,000 lb) thrust. In flight the wing-tip engines were switched off and the thrust of the Pegasus engines deflected back for normal cruising.

The Do-31 was a long way ahead of its time. Many problems, particularly that of the piercing noise gener-ated by the wing-tip engines, remain to be solved. (left)

ROCKWELL SPACE SHUTTLE

Up to now the exploration of space has been a very expensive business. This is partly due to the complex technical problems involved, and partly due to the fact that all spacecraft, both unmanned and manned, have only been used once and then scrapped.

The Space Shuttle is the first of a new generation of spacecraft designed to make repeated trips into space. It has a large cargo bay which can be used to carry satellites into orbit, or retrieve others which have either worn out or broken down, so that they can be brought back to Earth and overhauled. The bay can also be used to carry scientific equipment into orbit, or a small manned spacelab, in which experiments can be carried out.

In the nineteen-eighties the Space Shuttle will be making regular trips into space. On a clear night it will be visible from the surface of the earth just before sunrise and just after sunset. It will appear as a tiny point of light moving across the sky quite rapidly. By looking at its times of orbit, you will be able to see it and point it out, saying 'that was a Rockwell Space Shuttle'. (above)

LIGHT AIRCRAFT

Light aircraft, that is relatively small civil aircraft, outnumber all the military aircraft and airliners in the world combined. There are about 10,000 airliners throughout the world carrying passengers – but an estimated 200,000 light aircraft.

The term usually applied to these small aircraft is 'General Aviation', and covers aircraft used for pleasure, business, sport and agriculture.

Most of the light aircraft are in the United States, which has 150,000 out of the 200,000. There are also an estimated 750,000 private pilots in North America. Canada, a land of vast distances and great prosperity, has 50,000 pilots and 16,000 light aircraft. Many of these are in the northern territories, where there are few or no highways and railways. It is here that the 'Bush' pilots abound. This is the name given to the pilots who fly in those regions and acquire specialized knowledge about the local terrain and the weather, and who use special abilities to operate their aircraft in the harsh winter conditions. Bush aircraft often fly with skis in winter and floats in summer. Wheels may not be used at all.

The continent of Australia, another big country, has some 27,000 pilots and 4,000 aircraft. It is here that 'flying doctor' services are operated. As in parts of Africa and South America, sparse populations and poor or non-existent land transport make it impossible except by air to get medical help quickly to people who need it.

Private flying is very popular in France which has 37,000 pilots and 6,000 light aircraft. Britain, a relatively small country with a good network of roads and railways, has 20,000 pilots and 3,000 aircraft.

An important task undertaken by these General Aviation aircraft is that of agricultural flying. They are used to spray insecticides, fungicides and fertilizers. The demanding tasks of flying accurately very low has led to a range of specially-designed agricultural aircraft. A distinctive feature of these is the high set cockpit, designed to give the pilot the best possible view over the nose. The cockpit is also armoured to protect the pilot in the event of a crash. These happen quite often, but happily are rarely serious.

It has been estimated that there are about 24,000 agricultural aircraft in the world. They are used where the land is difficult to spray by any other method, and also because aerial treatment is relatively efficient. A single 'ag-plane' can treat more land in one hour than a tractor can do in a day, using only one-tenth of the fuel.

Agricultural aircraft are among the easiest of light aircraft to identify, because of their high-set cockpits and underwing spraybars. If one flies overhead, you should be able to tell 'what that plane is used for', even if you are unable to give it its proper name.

BEAGLE

The Pup, a two/three seat monoplane (*top*) and the B.206 five/eight seat twin-engined executive (*above*) were excellent products of the Beagle Company.

GRUMMAN AMERICAN CHEETAH

The Cheetah is a de-luxe four-seat cabin monoplane, typical of the many thousands of this type of 'flying motor car' so popular in America. Powered by a 150 hp Lycoming 'flat-four' engine, it has a top speed of 251 kmph (157 mph) and a range of 960 km (600 miles). (*centre right*)

DE HAVILLAND PUSS MOTH

I n spite of its relatively modern appearance, the Puss Moth is nearly fifty years old. Built in 1930, it was one of the first monoplanes built especially for private owners. It was a development of the Moth with which Britain pioneered the private aeroplane in 1925. In addition to the pilot the Puss Moth could carry two passengers in what at the time was regarded as great comfort. It cruised at just over 160 kmph (100 mph) and had a range of 480 km (300 miles).

It was a delightful aeroplane to fly and was well liked by its many pilots. (*below left*)

HANG GLIDER

H ang gliders are an increasingly common sight in hilly areas. These simple aircraft, under which the pilot sits or hangs from a trapeze, owe their development to Francis Rogallo. Rogallo's aim was to develop a kite the lift of which would equal that developed by an aeroplane wing. He began research in 1945.

In the 1950s and 1960s North American and Ryan (two American aircraft companies) experimented with these flex-wing kites, as they were called, as gliders and

advanced parachutes. One result was a flying jeep – the Fleep – which could lift quite heavy loads.

In the 1970s the hang glider has evolved. Basically, this is one of the simplest and cheapest flying machines ever invented, and has brought the thrill of flying within reach of many thousands of people who otherwise could never have afforded this most expensive of sports. (*above*)

CESSNA SKYMASTER

T he unusual layout of this four-to-six seat American aircraft resulted from several years' study by the Cessna company to produce a twin-engined aircraft that would be simple to fly, cheap to run, safe and comfortable.

In most 'planes, engines are mounted on the wings. If one fails, the pilot has very heavy loads to counteract swiftly if he is not to lose control, because the engine still working forces the plane to twist and turn.

On the Skymaster, with the engines in line, mounted at each end of the fuselage, this basic problem is eliminated. With its distinctive twin tail booms, the Skymaster is an easy aircraft to identify. If one flies overhead, you will be able to say 'That was a Cessna Skymaster'. (*top*)

ROCKWELL QUAIL COMMANDER

The Rockwell Quail Commander, built in Mexico, is typical of the light aircraft used for agricultural work. Like most aircraft specifically designed for this demanding work, it has a high-set armoured cockpit, to give the pilot an exceptionally good view over the nose, and to protect him in the event of a crash. The aircraft can spray either liquid or chemical fertilizers or insecticides. (*top*)

ROCKWELL SHRIKE COMMANDER

The Shrike Commander, a twin-engined, eight-seat aircraft, is typical of the many light aircraft in this class built for the business-man pilot and light freight work. All equipment can be removed to permit the cabin to be used for freight carrying.

The aircraft shown in the photograph is one used by the British Airports Authority for checking the elaborate system of navigation aids over the British Isles. (*left*)

PIERRE ROBIN DR 253 REGENT

The French-built Pierre Robin DR 253 Regent can seat up to five passengers and is one of the many light aircraft manufactured in Europe to challenge American domination in this highly-competitive market. (*above*)

CESSNA FLOATPLANE

This particular floatplane is used to carry rich commuters from their homes in Long Island to their offices in Wall Street, in New York.

Because the floats are quite heavy they drag the speed of the aeroplanes which therefore have lower performance that their wheeled counterparts.

However, there are many parts of the world, particularly in northern Canada and Alaska, in which level fields are rare and smooth runways even rarer. In these regions floatplanes are used in large numbers. (*top*)

HELICOPTERS

Helicopters are a very special kind of flying machine. On a normal aeroplane the wings are in fixed position and the lift is gained by propelling the wings, together with the fuselage and engine, through the air in the direction of travel. On a helicopter, however, the lift is obtained by spinning the wings, relative to the fuselage. This means that a helicopter can take-off and land vertically. This is the one major advantage of a helicopter over conventional aircraft. Helicopters however are relatively expensive to make and quite complicated mechanically so they are not as widely used as some people thought they would be.

The first manned helicopter, the Breguet-Richet No. 1 flew in September 1907, less than four years after the historic flight of the Wright Flyer on 17 December 1903.

It was not until the Sikorsky VS-300 flew in 1939, however, that the helicopter began to emerge as a practical aircraft.

There are two main reasons why it took so long.

One reason is that when a large rotor – the name given to the spinning wings of a helicopter – is turned mechanically, a force known as torque is generated which tends to make the fuselage rotate in the opposite direction. This would obviously be most disconcerting to the pilot and passengers. This problem can be overcome by using two rotors, spinning in opposite directions, to cancel this out. Alternatively, if a single rotor is used, a small tail rotor is usually fitted to counteract the torque.

The second reason presents a much bigger problem and concerns the lift generated by the rotor blades. In hovering flight, each rotor blade is moving through the air at the same speed and the same lift all the way round is developed. As soon as the helicopter begins to move forward, achieved by tilting the complete rotor in the direction of travel, the lift from each blade varies as it rotates. This is because on one side a blade is moving at its own speed plus the forward speed, while on the other side it is moving at its own speed minus the forward speed. The difference in lift generated can be sufficient to roll a helicopter right over, and this happened to many of the early machines built.

This problem is overcome by reducing the angle of the 'advancing' blade, (to reduce its lift) and increasing the angle of the 'retreating' blade, (to increase its lift), so that equal lift is generated both sides.

The mechanism which moves the blades up and down as they rotate is very complex and one reason

for the relatively high cost of helicopters.

From the Sikorsky VS-300, there developed during World War II, the R-4 and R-6, used for training, and the R-5, specially designed to be carried by cargo vessels and used for anti-submarine patrols. Only a few of these entered service, however, before the war ended.

Progress was slow after the war. It was the outbreak of war in Korea in 1950 that provided the next major boost to helicopter development. Helicopters were extensively used during this conflict to carry wounded soldiers away from the battlefield quickly to hospitals where their wounds could be treated properly. Their use saved the lives of many thousands of soldiers.

During the long bitter campaign in Vietnam, helicopters were used not only to evacuate the wounded, but also to carry soldiers and supplies right up to the front line and often beyond it. This war also saw the development of the helicopter gunship. This was a fast, heavily-armed helicopter, able to give close support and protection to troops moving into forward battle zones.

The advent of the turbine engine in the mid-1950s significantly assisted the development of the helicopter. They developed more power than the existing piston engines and were lighter. They also needed shorter warm-up periods before take-off and gave smoother operation in flight.

However, they did not make helicopters either simple or cheap. For a given power of engine and size, a fixed-wing aircraft of equivalent size and power could fly at about twice the speed and for about one third of the cost.

For this reason the use of helicopters tends to be restricted to duties which are not possible with fixed-wing aircraft.

At first sight many helicopters are so similar that to tell 'which helicopter that is' is not easy. Some helicopters, however, like the Sikorsky Skycrane, are so different that they can be identified easily.

However, like people, all helicopters are slightly different from each other, either in the shape of the fuselage, landing gear or rotor equipment. The differences in people enable a football fan to identify all the players of his favourite team. Similarly, a keen spotter should be able to answer the question 'What helicopter is that?'

BELL IROQUOIS

Nearly ten thousand of this effective 11–14 seat US military helicopter have been built since it entered service with the US Army in 1960. Over 15 major models have been built, the latest of which, the Model 214, can lift an external load of 3,175 kg (7,000 lb) on its cargo hook.

The Iroquois was used so extensively during the Vietnam War that some historians have already dubbed the conflict 'The Helicopter War'. (*top right*)

WESTLAND SEA KING

The Sea King was specially developed from the Sikorsky S-61 to provide Britain's Royal Navy with an advanced submarine hunter-killer helicopter able to stay aloft for prolonged patrols. The fuselage comprises a watertight hull which allows the machine to alight in the sea in an emergency. The main landing gear retracts into sponsons, which also have bouyancy bags to improve the boat-like capability of the helicopter on water.

The 'hunting' part of the Sea King's duties is carried out by advanced electronic equipment, including sonar sound-searching devices which are dipped into the sea, and the 'killing' part by either four depth charges or four homing torpedoes. (*centre right*)

WESTLAND LYNX

The Lynx was produced jointly by Britain and France and carried a bewildering array of guns, rockets and bombs, depth charges and homing torpedoes.

For Army strike missions a 20 mm cannon or a 7.62 mm Minigun pod can be fitted. For Navy attacks on small surface craft, four Sea Skua semi-active homing missiles or four wire-guided missiles can be carried. (*bottom right*)

The turbine engines are Pratt and Whitney PT6T-6 Twin Pac turboshaft, each developing sufficient lift for take-off. (*above*)

SIKORSKY S-6IN

The Sikorsky S-61 is a civil version of the US Navy HSS-2 and Marine HR35-1 helicopters. It can carry up to 30 passengers and cruises at 234 kmph (138 mph). The 61N version, shown in the photograph, has a sealed boat-like hull and outrigged floats to allow it to 'land' on and take off from calm water.

About 100 S-61Ns are in service all over the world. British Airways has a fleet of over twenty, and uses them to operate a service between Cornwall and the Scilly Isles, and to provide vital communication links with North Sea oil drilling rigs. (*left*)

SIKORSKY S-58T

This is a twin turbine-engined version of the original single piston-engined 12–18 seat S-58 helicopter which first appeared in 1954 and of which over 1,000 were built.

The turbine version provides increased safety and reliability, greater speed and lifting power and improved performance at high altitudes on hot days. The new version is also cheaper to run. It is used for both civil and military duties.

BELL HUEY COBRA

The Huey Cobra is a specially-developed helicopter 'gun-ship', designed to give close support and protection to troops in forward battle zones. Over 1,000 have been delivered to the US Army and the helicopter was extensively used in the war in Vietnam.

Armament includes a variety of rockets, mines, grenade launchers or machine gun pods mounted under the small stub wings, and a chin turret housing a Mini-gun six-barrel machine-gun with 8,000 rounds of ammunition, or a six-barrel 20 mm cannon with 1,000 rounds of ammunition. (*above*)

SIKORSKY SKYCRANE

As its name implies, this unusual helicopter is literally a flying crane, specially designed to carry bulky loads.

As can be seen from the photographs, unwieldy loads, like the pre-fabricated building, can be slung underneath on special lifting tackle, or a cargo pod can be secured directly below the centre section. The standard US Army pod can carry up to 45 troops or 24 stretchers, or bulky loads such as armoured cars, light tanks or small field guns, weighing up to 9,070 kg (20,000 lb). The Skycrane is driven by two powerful Pratt and Whitney turbine engines. (*right*)

BELL LONG RANGER

The main feature of this popular, seven-seat, general purpose light helicopter is the outstanding passenger comfort it offers. This comfort is achieved by the Bell Company's special Noda-Matic cabin suspension system. This system reduces the severe rotor-induced vibration, which is normally particularly noticeable at high speeds or when man-oeuvring, and helps to isolate the noise that comes from the structure itself. The result is a high degree of comfort normally associated with turbo-prop powered fixed-wing aircraft.

An executive version is available with an exceptionally luxurious cabin accommodating four passengers. (*above*)

AEROSPATIALE GAZELLE

An unusual feature of this Anglo-French helicopter is the housing of the tail rotor within a duct in the fin. This arrangement is known as a fenestron. The Gazelle was designed by Aerospatiale, but is made in both France and Britain.

It is used for light observation duties in the French, British and other armies, but military loads include anti-tank missiles, machine-guns, reconnaissance flares or smoke markers. More than 200 have been built. (*above*)

MIL V-12

In the 1960s, the Russian designer Mikhail Mil produced what was then the biggest helicopter in the world. Known as the Mi-6, it was powered by twin turbine engines each producing 5,500 shp, driving a huge rotor nearly 35 m (115 ft) in diameter.

The V-12 is twice this size, having been produced by using the Mi-6 power-units and rotors to lift a fuselage the size of a large airliner. The cavernous cargo compartment is over 27 m (90 ft) long by 4.2 m (14 ft) wide and high. Lifting capacity is nearly 40,082 kg (90,000 lb). (*left*)

WARPLANES

Two main types of warplane have been developed since the days of the Wright Flyer, one for fighting and one for bombing. In addition, numerous other types of aircraft have been built for military purposes, ranging from troop transports to helicopter gun-ships.

Fighters are the glamour 'planes of the sky. Powerful and manoeuvrable, they epitomize man's conquest of the air.

However, although machine-guns were fitted to aeroplanes as early as 1911, fighter 'planes developed slowly because there was no way of firing guns forward along the line of sight, without hitting the propeller. Early successes in World War I were achieved by pilots and observers who shot at enemy aeroplanes with revolvers and rifles, or with machine-guns mounted at an angle so that their bullets would not hit the propeller.

The invention of the interrupter gear solved this problem. As the name implies, this gear timed the bullets so that they passed between the blades of the propeller. Machine-guns could now be fitted parallel to the fuselage, making it much easier for the pilot to aim correctly.

Fighter plane development slowed with the return of peace. Gradually, however, biplanes gave way to monoplanes, retractable undercarriages were then introduced and cockpits were enclosed.

As many as eight machine-guns were installed on aircraft such as the Hawker Hurricane.

British fighter pilots achieved immortality during World War II, when in 1940 they won the vital Battle of Britain, this great victory being recorded for posterity by Sir Winston Churchill, British wartime Prime Minister with the words 'Never in the field of human conflict was so much owed by so many to so few.'

The development of the jet engine during this war gave the fighter a new lease of life, increasing its performance by a huge amount. Today, fighters fly at speeds approaching 3,210 kmph (2,000 mph) and can zoom to heights of 30,500 m (100,000 ft), and carry missiles which can destroy an enemy aircraft 160 km (100 miles) away.

Aircraft were used for bombing even before World War I. The Italians used them to drop bombs on their opponents in North Africa as early as 1911. It was World War I, however, that demonstrated the awesome potential of the bomb-carrying aeroplane. On 8 October 1914, two tiny Sopwith Tabloid biplanes made the first successful British air raid against Germany, destroying a new and secret Zeppelin. The bomber, however, did not come of age until World War II.

Since then extremely powerful thermo-nuclear bombs have been developed, which explode with a force equal to millions of tons of ordinary bombs.

Some of the exciting fighters and bombers developed during this period, and some specialized reconnaissance and transport aircraft, are described in this section of 'What Plane Is That?'.

CURTISS P40 WARHAWK

Nearly 14,000 examples of this fiercesome-looking American fighter were produced during World War II.

Some were sent to the Soviet Union where they became the first US fighters to see action on the Russian front. Others were shipped to China, where they equipped 'Flying Tiger' units. Many were used in the Middle East by the Royal Air Force, who called them Tomahawks.

It was not an outstanding fighter, but it was rugged and carried out less important duties well. (*top*)

FAIREY SWORDFISH

A carrier-borne, torpedo-spotter-reconnaissance biplane, the Swordfish is one of the best-remembered British warplanes used in World War II.

In spite of its ancient look, it performed so well under battle conditions, that it actually outlasted the aeroplane specially designed to replace it – the Albacore.

Stringbags, as the Swordfish was affectionately

known, were used in a spectacular attack on the Italian fleet at Taranto, which knocked out three battleships, a cruiser, two destroyers and two auxiliary ships, altering the balance of power in the Mediterranean during a critical period of the war. Swordfish also took part in the sinking of the formidable German battleship, the *Bismarck*. (*above and right*)

GLOSTER GLADIATOR

The Gloster Gladiator of 1934 is typical of the advanced biplane fighters which appeared in the 1930s just before the introduction of the faster and more formidable monoplane fighters.

It was the first Royal Air Force fighter to be armed with four machine-guns and, powered by a 840 hp Bristol Mercury engine, it had a top speed of over 402 kmph (250 mph).

Four Sea Gladiators based at Malta, three of them said to have been individually named *Faith*, *Hope* and *Charity*, won immortal fame by defending the island alone during the month of June 1940 against fierce attacks launched by the Italian Air Force. (*top right*)

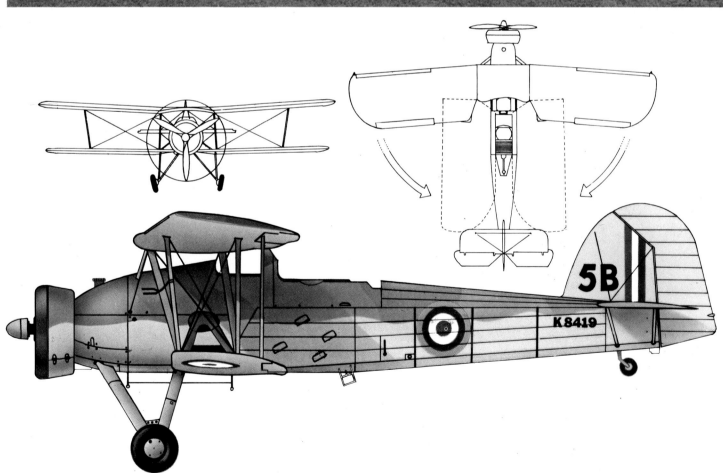

31

BOEING P26A

The Boeing P-26 first entered service with the US Army Air Corps in 1934. It was the first American monoplane fighter and one of the fastest of its day, with a top flight of 378 kmph (234 mph). It became known as the 'peashooter' and was powered by a 600 hp Pratt & Whitney Wasp engine. It was used in China in the 1930s and in the Philippines in 1941–2.

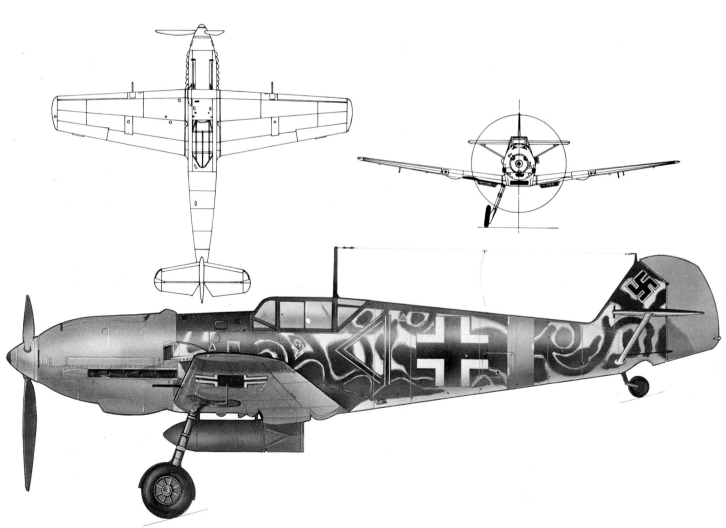

MESSERSCHMITT Bf 109

The Bf 109 was the standard single-seat fighter of the German Luftwaffe during the first half of World War II.

However, it saw service before then, during the Spanish Civil War in 1937 and it remained in production, somewhere in the world, for a remarkable 25 years, during which time about 35,000 were built. This huge production figure exceeds that of any other warplane, and for this reason alone, the Bf 109 is assured of a permanent niche in warplane history.

During the early years of World War II, the Bf 109's fine performance and excellent manoeuvrability proved superior against all opposing types of fighter throughout Poland, Czechoslovakia, France, Belgium, Holland and Britain – with the exception of the Spitfire. (*left*)

HAWKER HURRICANE

The Hurricane was not the fastest fighter of its day. Enemy aircraft such as Germany's Messerschmitt Bf 109 could out-dive it. The Hurricane fuselage was covered with old-fashioned fabric rather than the metal used by some other aircraft. Other fighters could fly higher.

It was, however, as far as Britain was concerned, the right fighter, in the right place, at the right time. The time was the summer of 1940 when Britain alone faced the might of Germany's Luftwaffe. The Royal Air Force won the ensuing Battle and so set the Allies on the path to eventual victory.

The Hurricane was powered by a Rolls-Royce Merlin engine which gave it a useful speed of about 520 kmph (325 mph) and excellent manoeuvrability. Its heavy armament of eight machine-guns caused severe damage to the lightly armoured German bombers which attacked Britain. (*above*)

AVRO LANCASTER

The Lancaster was the most successful of the heavy bombers flown by the Royal Air Force in World War II. It has been estimated that for each of these aircraft lost in action a record 132 tons of bombs were dropped, and it was the only Allied bomber capable of carrying the massive 9,978 kg (22,000 lb) Grand Slam bomb from bases in Britain to targets in Germany.

Over 7,000 Lancasters were built. Pictured is the last airworthy Lancaster (PA 474) of the RAF. Christened *City of Lincoln*, it bears the codes of 44 Squadron, the first to fly the type. (*top and centre*)

HEINKEL HeIII

Although designed as a bomber, many early versions of this German aircraft were completed as ten-seat airliners in order to try and convince people that it was a purely peaceful venture.

It first saw service in the Spanish Civil War, where its excellent performance enabled it to outrun opposing fighters.

The He III was in front line service somewhere in the world from 1937 to the late 1960s, a record equalled by few other warplanes. (*right*)

36

DE HAVILLAND MOSQUITO

Built of wood in order to use the skills of British furniture makers and to avoid the use of scarce metals, the Mosquito was one of the outstanding British warplanes of World War II.

It was designed primarily as a light bomber and used its high speed of nearly 640 kmph (400 mph) to evade enemy fighters rather than defensive armament. Only one Mosquito was lost for every 2,000 sorties, the lowest by far of any bomber used by Bomber Command.

Mosquitos destroyed one V-1 Flying Bomb site for every 40 tons of bombs dropped, compared with 219 tons from Mitchells, 182 tons from Marauders and 165 tons from Flying Fortresses.

When fitted with guns it proved to be a formidable fighter, and with cameras installed it was used extensively for reconnaissance purposes. (*above*)

NORTH AMERICAN MUSTANG

During the summer months, if you hear a deep-throated throb in the sky, it may come from one of these American fighters of World War II. A number of them are often flown at air shows.

The throb comes from the American-built Rolls-Royce Merlin engine. Delivering 1,590 hp, this engine, together with the high aerodynamic efficiency of the wing, gave the fighter a top speed of 703 kmph (437 mph) and a range of 2,655 km (1,650 miles).

This long range enabled the Mustang to be one of the best escort fighters of the war.

Distinguishing features of the Mustang are its straight-edged, slightly-tapered wing and bulging radiator under the middle of the fuselage. In the photograph the radiator is partly hidden by the fairing on the undercarriage leg. (*top*)

FOCKE-WULF FW-190

This snub-nosed German fighter was one of the outstanding combat aircraft of World War II. It was fast and manoeuvrable, it had good performance at both low and high altitudes, it was pleasant to fly and steady when firing its guns or dropping bombs. A distinctive feature of the design was the exceptionally neat cowling of the powerful radial engine, a feature later copied on many other aircraft. The fighter remained in production for six years during which more than 20,000 were built.

The basic armament was two cannon and two machine-guns. As a fighter-bomber it could carry a 1,814 kg (4,000 lb) bomb. (*above*)

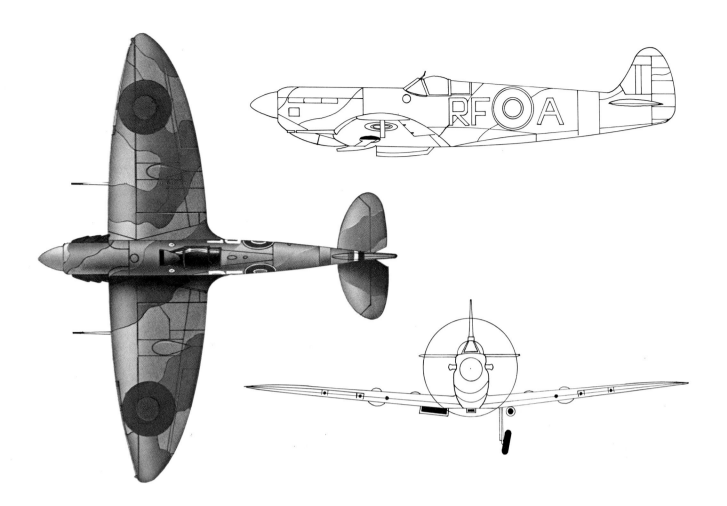

MESSERSCHMITT Me 262

This German fighter of World War II was the first jet propelled warplane to go into squadron service anywhere in the world.

Two revolutionary turbojet engines gave the fighter a top speed of 869 kmph (540 mph), and the main armament was four 30 mm cannons. This combination of high speed and heavy armament made the Me 262 a formidable fighter indeed.

Fortunately for the Allies, production was delayed, partly by the devastation caused by a heavy bombing raid on the Messerschmitt factory and partly by an instruction by Hitler to modify the fighter so that it could carry bombs.

The result was that the aircraft went into service too late to have any significant effect on the air battles of World War II. (*bottom left*)

Two major versions became operational, the first being the basic interceptor, the Me 262A-1a Swalbe (Swallow) armed with four 30 mm cannons, although several subversions had other armourment installations including rocket projectiles. The second version was the Me 262-2a Sturmvogel (Stormbird) fighter-bomber which could carry two 550 lb bombs beneath the fuselage.

SUPERMARINE SPITFIRE

Many historians consider the sleek Spitfire the greatest combat aircraft ever built. It was certainly the most famous fighter of World War II, when the distinctive eliptical wings enabled ordinary people in their millions to say very definitely 'That is a Spitfire'.

Together with its partner fighter the Hurricane, it achieved immortal fame when, during the vital Battle of Britain in 1940, it stood up to and overcame, the furious Luftwaffe attacks on England.

Powered by a Rolls-Royce Merlin engine, it had a maximum speed of 602 kmph (374 mph) and its manoeuvrability gave it a decisive edge over opposing German fighters, including the formidable Focke-Wulf FW-190. The armament varied, but most Spitfires had two 20 mm cannon and four machine-guns.

To counter the threat posed by low-level fighter-bomber versions of the Focke-Wolfe FW-190, Spitfires were fitted with Griffon engines designed to develop their maximum power near the ground.

Over 20,000 Spitfires were built, and over 2,000 of its naval counterpart, the Seafire. Few survive today, however, so you will be lucky indeed to see one in the air. (*above and centre left*)

MESSERSCHMITT Me 163

This was Germany's revolutionary rocket-powered fighter whose speed of 960 kmph (600 mph) was much higher than that of any Allied aircraft. The rocket engine also gave the Me 163 a phenomenal rate of climb, but used fuel so quickly that after climbing up to the height of its target, the fighter could fly for only another 2½ minutes. After carrying out its attack the Me 163 glided down to land, a hazardous procedure which often resulted in the aircraft catching fire and the death of the pilot. Like other German advanced fighters, the Me 163 was too late and not produced in sufficient numbers to have a major effect on the outcome of World War II (*above*)

BOEING B-17 FLYING FORTRESS

This famous American bomber of World War II, earned the nickname 'Flying Fortress' because of its heavy defensive armament. This included twin 0.50-inch machine guns in the tail, two in a power-operated front upper turret, two in a most unusual 'ball' turret under the fuselage, and single guns firing through apertures in each side of the fuselage. Some aircraft had two extra guns, firing forward, in a 'chin' turret under the nose.

Flying Fortresses were used in hundreds to make heavy raids in daylight on targets deep inside Germany and occupied Europe. During these missions they flew in tight formations so that the guns of several aircraft could be brought to bear on any attacking fighters. Running battles were fought as the bombers flew towards their targets and again on the way back to their bases. Heavy losses were suffered by both the bombers and the opposing fighters.

The photograph shows one of the 3,400 B-17Fs that were built. (*left*)

CONVAIR B-36

This giant American bomber was designed in 1941, when the US Army Air Force had to face the possibility of having to attack targets in Europe from bases in North America.

To meet the need, the Air Force decided to commission an aircraft able to fly 8,000 km (5,000 miles) with a 4,536 kg (10,000 lb) bomb load and then return to its base cruising at about 400 kmph (250 mph) at 10,668 m (35,000 ft).

The result was the B-36, powered by six Pratt and Whitney Wasp Major piston engines, buried in the 6-ft thick wing and driving pusher propellers.

The war ended before the first B-36 flew, on 8 August 1946. About 100 were built however. To boost the speed to 700 kmph (435 mph) and the operating ceiling to 13,716 m (45,000 ft), Convair added four turbojet engines, mounted as two pairs, in pods under the wing. The aircraft could carry two 19,050 kg (42,000 lb) 'Grand Slam' bombs. With its unusual 'pusher' propellers, the B-36 was an easy aeroplane for people to say what 'plane that was. (*inset left*)

BOEING B-29 SUPERFORTRESS

The heaviest warplane built during World War II, the Superfortress was extensively used in the air attacks against Japan.

Four powerful Wright Cyclone engines, each developing 2,200 hp, gave the sleek bomber a top speed of 576 kmph (357 mph) and a range of over 6,400 km (4,000 miles). The normal bomb load was 5,443 kg (12,000 lb). It was defended by up to 10 machine-guns and one cannon, most of them mounted in remotely-controlled turrets.

The B-29 is assured of a place in history as it was the aircraft used for the only two atomic bomb attacks of World War II, Hiroshima on 6 August 1945 and Nagasaki on 14 August 1945. Had the war continued many hundreds of thousands of lives could have been lost during a conventional invasion by troops from boats.

In 1979 the only airworthy example of a B-29 is with the Confederate Air Force.

DOUGLAS SKYRAIDER

Designed during World War II as a dive-bomber and torpedo attack aircraft, Skyraider was just too late to see service during this war.

However, over 3,000 were built and the Skyraider saw extensive action during the Korean War, where its ability to carry an enormous range of bombs and rockets from as many as fifteen points under the wing and fuselage, made it an ideal ground-attack aircraft. In spite of the use of advanced jet fighter-bombers, such as the Phantom and Corsair, in Vietnam, the Skyraider was also extensively used in this conflict, where its relatively low speed often proved better for dropping bombs accurately on difficult targets. (*top left*)

GLOSTER METEOR

The Meteor was the only Allied jet aircraft to see action in World War II.

It was powered by two engines as the types of turbojet available at the time were not powerful enough for the required performance to be obtained from only one engine.

Early Meteors had a top speed of only 656 kmph (410

44

mph), but later types, with more powerful engines, had a speed of 926 kmph (579 mph). For such an early design the Meteor proved very versatile, being developed into a two-seat trainer, a photo-reconnaissance aircraft and a two-seat, all-weather night fighter.

The Meteor achieved its first success on 4 August 1944, when a pilot whose guns had jammed, destroyed a V-1 flying-bomb by flying alongside and tipping it out of control with his wing tip. (*top right*)

HAWKER HUNTER

The Hunter is a single-seat day fighter. Although it cannot fly as fast as the speed of sound in level flight, it has such good handling qualities that it remains in service with a number of air forces today – twenty-five years after it first went into service with the Royal Air Force.

It is armed with air-to-air missiles and four hard-hitting 30 mm Aden cannon. To make re-arming easier the guns are mounted in a detachable pack containing the gun-bodies and ammunition magazines. After a sortie this can be removed and a loaded pack fitted in a few minutes.

The clean lines of this superbly streamlined warplane are evident from the photograph. (*left*)

NORTH AMERICAN F-86 SABRE

Few aircraft have become a legend in their own time. The F-86 Sabre is one of the few.

Designed initially to have straight wings, a swept-wing arrangement was adopted when a study of German research documents, captured at the end of World War II, indicated that this would greatly improve the performance. This decision gave the Sabre a top speed of 1,086 kmph (675 mph) and turned a mediocre fighter into a great one.

The testing time for the Sabre came in the 1950s when, during the Korean War, it came up against Russia's formidable MiG-15. Although initially outgunned, the Sabre had slight superiority in certain aspects of performance which the battle-hardened US pilots exploited to great advantage. The result was that for each Sabre lost in combat at least four MiG-15s were shot down.

Shown in the photograph is an F-86D, a rocket-armed variant used for the defence of America and Europe. Today, thirty years after its conception, pilots still remember the superb flying qualities of the Sabre. (*above*)

46

NORTH AMERICAN F-100 SUPER SABRE

The Super Sabre was a logical development of the very successful Sabre, and was originally known as the Sabre 45 because the wing sweep angle was increased to 45 degrees. By the time the design was finalized, however, little resemblance to the Sabre remained. An unusual flattened nose intake makes the F-100 an easy aircraft to identify.

With a top speed of 1,232 kmph (770 mph), the Super Sabre was the first US fighter able to fly faster than the speed of sound in level flight. This step into the unknown of supersonic flight resulted in control difficulties which led to a series of accidents and the aircraft was grounded while modifications were carried out.

With the snags ironed out the F-100, armed with four 20 mm cannon and air-to-air rockets, was a good fighter. For use as a fighter-bomber, it could carry a variety of bombs and rockets weighing up to 3,401 (7,500 lb) under its wings. (*right*)

REPUBLIC F-84 THUNDERJET

One of America's early jet fighters, the Thunderjet just failed to see service during World War II. However, it made a name for itself during the Korean War, being particularly effective for ground-attack duties. For such missions it could carry up to 1,814 kg (4,000 lb) of bombs and rockets. It could also carry a nuclear bomb, but never dropped one of these 'Doomsday' weapons in anger.

Powered by a 1,814 kg (4,000 lb) thrust General Electric engine, the Thunderjet had a top speed of around 960 kmph (600 mph). It was the last straight-winged, subsonic fighter to be used operationally by the US Air Force. (*above*)

DASSAULT SUPER MYSTÈRE

The Super Mystère was the final development of a series of single-seat fighters developed during the 1950s.

The Mystère II was the first French aircraft to fly faster than the speed of sound, which it achieved in a dive in October 1958. Next to appear in the Mystère series was the Mystère IV, originally known as the Super Mystère, which had smaller wings and a larger fuselage.

The final aircraft, the Super Mystère, had thinner and more sharply-swept wings, with a 'saw-tooth' leading edge, and a flatter nose to improve the pilot's field of view. Standard armament was two 30 mm cannon and a fuselage pack of 55 air-to-air rockets. (*top*)

LOCKHEED F-104 STARFIGHTER

Sometimes described as a 'missile with a man in it', the distinguishing feature of this single-seat American fighter is its relatively small, razor-edged wings.

When it was first produced it had an outstanding performance and held three world records for speed and altitude. It was the first fighter to be armed with the Vulcan 20 mm cannon, a Gatling type of gun with six barrels and a devastating rate of fire. This is a most awesome weapon for ground-strafing missions. For air combat the aircraft carries Sidewinder missiles.

The photograph shows a Starfighter during 'zero-length' take-off tests for the German Air Force at Edwards Air Force Base. The solid fuel rocket motor under the fuselage propelled the fighter into the air up to flying speed and was then jettisoned. (*centre left*)

TUPOLEV TU-20

When asked 'What 'plane is that?' heading unannounced towards Britain, the pilot of the RAF Phantom in the photograph went up to look and reported 'A Russian Tupolev TU-20, code named Bear'.

Initially designed as a long range heavy bomber, the TU-20 is now used primarily for reconnaissance duties. It regularly monitors shipping around the British Isles, oil drilling activities in the North Sea, and NATO naval manoeuvres in the Atlantic. It is powered by four power-ful turbo-prop engines, each developing 15,000 hp, and giving the giant aircraft a range of around 10,800 km (8,000 miles).

However, if you see a large swept-wing aircraft powered by four turbo-prop engines, think before you say 'that plane was a Bear'. It is more likely to be a TU-114, a passenger-carrying airliner based on the Bear, with a bigger fuselage. (*bottom left*)

ENGLISH ELECTRIC LIGHTNING

The Lightning was the first single seater fighter that was able to exceed the sound barrier in level flight. It can fly at Mach 2 (twice the speed of sound) with a ceiling of 18,290 metres (60,000 feet). The thrust of its two Rolls-Royce engines can be increased to 6,545 kilogrammes (14,430 lb) by afterburning, but as this increases fuel consumption and therefore shortens the range of the 'plane, it is only used for a few seconds at at time. (*above*)

SAAB VIGGEN

This powerful Swedish warplane is one of the easiest fighters to recognize because of its unusual wing layout.

Known as a 'canard configuration', it has a small wing, the 'foreplane' in front of the main wing, instead of the normal tail surface behind the wing as on conventional aircraft.

The unusual layout helps the Viggen to take-off well, and it can in fact operate from relatively short stretches of straight motor-way.

The fighter can carry a wide range of bombs, and Sidewinder missiles or gun pods, on three attachment points under each wing. The Viggen has a maximum level speed of just over 960 kmph (600 mph). (*top*)

ENGLISH ELECTRIC CANBERRA

This finely-streamlined aircraft was one of the most successful bombers of the 1950s. It was the first jet bomber to serve with the Royal Air Force.

It became famous for its fighter-like climbs and tight turns at air shows, and earned the distinction of being the only modern British aircraft to be built under licence in the United States, where it was manufactured by the Martin Company and designated the B-57. An unusual feature of the American-built bomber was a rotary bomb door.

The good high-flying performance of the Canberra led to the development of a special reconnaissance version with a new long-span wing. The British version could cruise at 18,288 m (60,000 ft). The US Air Force developed the aircraft further. With an even bigger wing, the American reconnaissance version could cruise at 45,359 m (100,000 ft). (*centre left*)

DASSAULT-DORNIER ALPHA-JET

It is no good having the best warplanes in the world, if there are no trained pilots to fly them.

The outcome of many conflicts has been determined more by the skill of the pilots involved than a marked superiority in aircraft performance. Such conflicts include the war in Korea, where the superior skill of the Sabre pilots overcame the relatively poorly trained pilots of the opposing MiGs, and the Middle East wars, where the outstanding skill of Israeli pilots has overcome enemy air forces vastly superior numerically.

The design of a training aircraft is not quite as simple as it may seem. The aircraft must be easy to fly and must not react too violently if the student pilot makes a mistake. But it must not be too easy nor too forgiving, otherwise the pilots could not gain the skills required to fly more advanced aircraft.

Many pilots consider that in the Alpha Jet, a new advanced training aircraft being produced jointly by France and Germany, the right balance has been obtained. (*bottom left*)

LOCKHEED U-2

Looking something like a slender-winged sailplane, the U-2 is, in fact, a long-range, high-altitude reconnaissance aircraft, able to fly 6,400 km (4,000 miles) at 21,336 m (70,000 ft).

The aircraft was built in the Lockheed company's famous secret 'Skunk' works in Burbank. The U stood for 'Utility', one of the many steps taken to disguise the real purpose of the aircraft.

In 1955 President Eisenhower proposed an 'Open Skies' scheme whereby the United States and Russia would allow the other to make reconnaissance flights to provide proof that no plans were being made for a surprise attack. The Russian president rejected the proposal, but America, suspicious of Russia's excessive secrecy, made flights over the Soviet Union. In 1960 a U-2 was shot down while photographing long-range missile bases under construction in Russia. The pilot, Gary Powers, bailed out and was captured. At his trial it was revealed that the U-2 could take 8000 photographs covering an area 160 km (100 miles) wide by 3,520 km (2,200 miles) long. Today, U-2s are used for high altitude weather reconnaissance flights. (*top*)

BLACKBURN BUCCANEER

The Buccaneer is a two-seat, twin-engined, low-level, high-speed strike and reconnaissance aircraft in service with the Royal Navy, the Royal Air Force and the South African Air Force.

Its relatively small size tends to hide a truly spectacular performance, much of which is still secret. Its radius of action, however, is in the neighbourhood of 1,600 km (1,000 miles) and the maximum bomb load is 7,257 kg (16,000 lb).

Part of the excellent performance is due to the application of what is known as the 'area rule' design technique to the fuselage, giving it a coke-bottle shape, which delays the drag rise near the speed of sound. Low take-off and landing speeds are achieved by the use of boundary layer control over the wing leading edge, drooped ailerons, flaps and tailplanes. The lower speed makes the Buccaneer easier and safer to land.

DASSAULT MIRAGE 5

The delta-winged Mirage 5 is a ground attack aircraft especially designed so that they are simple to maintain and able to operate from rough airfields. It can carry up to 3,991 kg (8,800 lb) of bombs and 1,000 litres (220 gallons) of fuel under the wing and fuselage in addition to its internal armament of two 30 mm cannon.

The Mirage 5 can fly at twice the speed of sound and can also be used as an interceptor, for which purpose it can carry two Sidewinder air-to-air missiles and 4,545 litres (1,000 gallons) of fuel externally. (*top*)

DASSAULT MIRAGE 50

The Mirage 50 is one of a large family of delta-winged fighters and bombers made by the French company Dassault, and which now serve in many air forces all over the world.

The Mirage 50 is a multi-mission fighter, suitable for air superiority duties with cannon and missiles, air patrol, supersonic interception and ground attack. It can carry the formidable range of bombs and rockets developed for earlier Mirages. Compared with other aircraft in the family, the -50 has a better take-off performance, a higher rate of climb, faster acceleration and better manoeuvrability.

The delta wing is a distinctive feature on this aircraft, but be careful before you say 'that 'plane was a Mirage 50' as other fighters also have wings of this shape, because it is a good one for supersonic flight. (*above*)

VOUGHT A-7 CORSAIR

The A-7A Corsair is a standard US Navy carrier-based fighter-bomber. The A-7D is the US Air Force counterpart, developed into a tactical fighter.

The Corsair programme evolved from a US Navy requirement for a single-seat carrier-based light attack aircraft to replace the Douglas A-4 Skyhawk. To keep costs to a minimum and to speed delivery, the US Navy stipulated that the new aircraft should be based on an existing design. LTV (Ling-Temco-Vought) now Vought, won the competition with a design based on the Crusader.

Originally, the Corsair was designed to carry 4,535 kg (10,000 lb) of bombs, but the latest versions can carry up to 6,803 kg (15,000 lb) on six under-wing pylons and two fuselage weapon stations. In addition, a Vulcan cannon is mounted in the left side of the fuselage. This fearsome weapon has a rate of fire of 6,000 rounds per minute. (*right*)

BRITISH AEROSPACE HARRIER

The Harrier was the first V/STOL fighter to go into service in the world, the initials standing for Vertical/Short Take-off and Landing. The ability to take-off and land vertically makes Harrier fighter squadrons independent of vulnerable fixed bases, being able to operate from jungle clearings, beaches, roads, or the decks of ships at sea.

The ability to take-off and land vertically is given by two rotating exhaust nozzles attached to each side of the 9,752 kg (21,500 lb) thrust Pegasus turbofan engine. By diverting the exhaust downwards, these enable the

Harrier to rise vertically by the jet-lift technique. At a safe height, the pilot rotates the nozzles slowly to obtain forward thrust as well as lift. When the aircraft is flying fast enough for the wings to provide sufficient lift to support it, the nozzles are rotated fully rearward, so that all the engine thrust is used for propulsion. Landing is the reverse of take-off.

In addition to their primary function of deflecting thrust for vertical take-offs and landings, the nozzles can also be used to great effect in dog-fights. By deflecting the nozzles during combat, an extraordinary degree of manoeuvrability can be obtained. The effectiveness of the technique of using the nozzles in this manner has been demonstrated in simulated dog-fights against such famous aircraft as the Grumman F-14 Tomcat, in which

at heights of up to 6,096 m (20,000 ft), the Harrier came out on top. Of interest is the fact that during a typical dog-fight, lasting say three minutes, the Harrier uses only about 273 litres (60 gallons) of fuel. A conventional fighter uses at least 2½ times as much fuel. The aircraft which 'breaks-off' and starts to fly home first is usually the first one to be shot down in these days of homing missiles!

No weapons are carried internally on the Harrier, the combat load being carried on four underwing and one underfuselage pylons. A typical combat load is a pair of 30 mm Aden gun-pods, a 454-kg (1,000-lb) bomb on the under-fuselage pylon, a 454-kg (1,000-lb) bomb on each of the inboard wing pylons and a rocket pod containing nineteen 68 mm rockets on each outboard pylon.

LOCKHEED SR-71 BLACKBIRD

Built in secret at the famous Lockheed 'Skunk Works' in Burbank, the Blackbird is the pride and joy of the US Air Force fleet of reconnaissance aircraft.

Constructed mainly in titanium, the Blackbird can cruise at Mach 3, that is, three times the speed of sound, at a height of over 24,384 m (80,000 ft), for 4,828 km (3,000 miles). It is packed with cameras, radars and infra-red sensors which can map 155,399sq.km (60,000 sq. miles) in an hour. Its missions include keeping a watch on movements of Russian naval fleets and on probable trouble spots such as the Middle East.

In 1978 Blackbird held several world air records, including the coveted 'speed in a straight line' which it gained on 28 July 1976 by flying over a measured course at 3,529 kmph (2,193 mph). (*above*)

McDONNELL DOUGLAS F-4 PHANTOM

The F-4E Phantom was introduced in 1967 and has a 20-mm multi-barrel, rapid-fire gun and a slatted wing. It can carry Maverick air-to-ground missile which can be guided with pinpoint accuracy by television, infra-red and laser beam. (*right*)

58

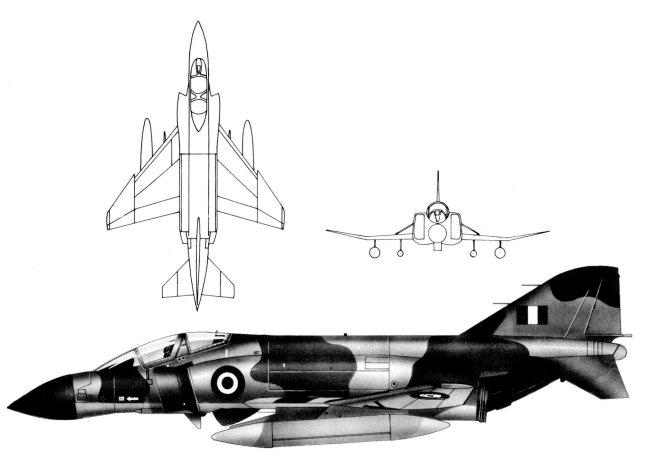

GENERAL DYNAMICS F-111

This formidable fighter-bomber was the first military aircraft to have a swing-wing. For take-off and landing, the wings are spread, to provide maximum lift. For high speed flight of up to two-and-a-half-times the speed of sound, the wings are swept back to provide minimum drag. This swing-wing feature is now commonly embodied on many modern warplanes.

The F-111 is armed with a multi-barrel 20 mm cannon and two special bombs in an internal weapon bay. In addition, six nuclear bombs, or a variety of rockets can be carried on three pylons under each wing, giving a maximum weapon load of fifteen tons. The two inboard pylons pivot as the wings sweep back to keep the bombs or rockets parallel to the fuselage. The outboard pylon does not swivel and is jettisoned if the wings are swept back. (*below and right*)

McDONNELL DOUGLAS F-15 EAGLE

Because the cost of developing modern warplanes is so high, air forces often use what are known as 'multi-role' aircraft, that is, 'planes able to perform more than one mission.

An aircraft specially designed for one specific mission, however, will usually be able to do this better than one designed for several missions. The Eagle is a specialized 'air superiority' fighter, that is, it is specifically designed for air-to-air combat. For this duty it has an outstanding performance and is exceptionally manoeuvrable. It is armed with a 20 mm six-barrel cannon, and four Sparrow and four Sidewinder missiles.

This does not mean that the Eagle cannot also be used to attack targets on the ground. Five weapon stations allow it to carry up to 7,264 kg (16,000 lb) of bombs. When these have been released, the Eagle once again becomes what is probably the world's best 'dog-fight' combat aircraft.

Eagles are currently engaged on air defence interceptor duties on the Atlantic coast, for which purpose they carry live ammunition and missiles. (*top*)

SEPECAT JAGUAR

This Anglo-French fighter is in wide scale service in Europe with the British and French Air Forces.

Designed for tactical support duties, that is for attacking ground targets to assist Allied army units, it can carry a quite amazing load of bombs, rockets and guns, weighing up to a total of 4,536 kg (10,000 lb).

Jaguars in service with the French Air Force can carry bombs and rockets with atomic warheads. The Royal Air Force operates a special reconnaissance version with a large pod containing cameras and infra-red equipment.

Shown in the photograph is a Jaguar International, a special export version with more powerful engines giving a speed of nearly 1,600 kmph (1,000 mph). (*left*)

HANDLEY PAGE VICTOR

The Victor is quite easily recognizable because of its distinctive crescent-shaped wings. It was introduced in the mid-1950s as one of the RAF's three V-bombers capable of carrying nuclear weaponry. The other two were the Vickers Valiant and the Avro Vulcan.

PANAVIA TORNADO

The Tornado, which was developed jointly by Britain, Germany and Italy, is an advanced, twin-engined, two-seat, supersonic, multi-role combat aircraft.

It is designed to undertake no less than six important roles: close air support, air superiority, counter air strike, interception, naval strike and reconnaissance. The same aircraft cannot actually undertake all these missions, but the same basic airframe, fitted with different equipment and weapons, can.

It is not easy to design one airframe that can do all these things, and the necessary fundamental flexibility of the Tornado is obtained by the use of a swing-wing. Spread straight, these provide maximum lift and enable the aircraft to carry a heavy warload from relatively small airfields. In flight the wings can be swept back for minimum drag and maximum speed. The special under-wing pylons rotate as the wing sweep is altered, so that bombs or other stores are always pointing in the line of flight.

The Tornado fixed armament is two newly-developed 27 mm cannon, and bombs, rockets, mines and other weapons can be carried under the wings and fuselage. (*above*)

ROCKWELL OV-10 BRONCO

This rather unusual twin-boomed turbo-prop warplane was specially designed for low-level reconnaissance missions and for ground-attack duties in what are often referred to as minor or 'brush' wars.

The large windows give good visibility, and for ground attack the Bronco is armed with two machine-guns in unusual sponsons extending from the fuselage, to which can be attached a variety of bombs, missiles and flares. (*left*)

FOLLAND GNAT

The Gnat is a single-seat, lightweight fighter, designed to be simple and to halt the trend towards ever heavier, ever more complicated and ever more expensive fighters. With a wing span of 6 m (22 ft) and weighing 3,016 kg (6,650 lb), it was only one third the size and about half the weight of conventional contemporary fighters.

Unfortunately, the venture was seriously delayed in the early stages when development of the original engine around which the aircraft had been designed was abandoned. Two years passed before another suitable engine became available, and when the Gnat finally appeared, its combat effectiveness was questionable, as it was not able to carry the extensive and bulky electronic equipment considered by many to be essential for the location and destruction of fast, high-flying targets.

A two-seat trainer version is in service with the Royal Air Force and a special aerobatic team of these, known as the Red Arrows, has delighted audiences all over the world with spectacular shows of unequalled precision flying, due both to the high skill of the pilots and the really excellent flying characteristics of the aircraft.

SAAB DRAKEN

The plans for this Swedish fighter demanded an interceptor with a high sub-sonic speed, a fast climb to a high altitude, good manoeuvrability at all heights, the ability to carry a heavy load of varied bombs and rockets and the ability to take-off and land on small airfields.

To meet these demanding requirements an unusual double-delta wing was chosen. The inner portion is sharply swept at 80° to give minimum drag at high speeds, while the outer section is swept at 57° to give good stability and handling at low speeds. This distinctive feature makes it easy to tell whether or not 'that 'plane was a Draken'. (*top*)

GRUMMAN F-14 TOMCAT

The F-14 Tomcat is a supersonic carrier-based fighter designed to fulfil three main missions.

The first of these, fighter-escort duties, involves clearing battlefield airspace of enemy fighters.

The second mission, known as CAP, standing for Combat Air Patrol, involves defending naval fleet task forces.

The third mission, interdiction, involves the attack of tactical, that is battlefield, targets on the ground.

Bearing in mind the severe conditions which would exist in a 'shooting-war', in order to accomplish these three missions the Tomcat is a complicated and expensive aircraft.

To provide the necessary performance, it not only has swing-wings, but also small foreplanes, called glove-vanes, which extend from the leading edge automatically at supersonic speed to control the shift of the centre-of-pressure. Two Pratt and Whitney afterburning turbofan engines, each developing 9,480 kg (20,900 lb) thrust, provide the power.

Piloting an advanced aircraft is a complicated business, without the extra burden of tracking and identifying enemy aircraft while having to overcome electronic jamming. Thus, in addition to the pilot, the Tomcat carries a weapons systems operator.

The standard armament is a Vulcan, multi-barrel, 20 mm cannon in the fuselage, four Sparrow air-to-air missiles which are under the fuselage and four Phoenix

missiles positioned under the wings.

The Phoenix missiles are controlled by an extremely advanced radar system, which can track up to 24 hostile targets at once – without alerting them to the fact that they are being 'watched'. When the time comes to attack, the system can launch up to six missiles, from over 160 km (100 miles), at six separate targets, and still keep an eye on 24 more. As the Phoenix missile closes on its target, its own radar takes over. Nothing can out-manoeuvre the Phoenix.

The Tomcat is indeed an expensive aircraft. It is, however, a great deal cheaper than the war it is helping to prevent. (*above left*)

GENERAL DYNAMICS F-16

The F-16 is a very manoeuvrable single-seat fighter with an impressive rate of climb. Its basic armament is a rapid-firing 20 mm multi-barrel cannon mounted internally and two infra-red air-to-air missiles on the wing tips.

A special flying control system helps to make the F-16 extremely manoeuvrable. Instead of the usual mechanical linkage of cables and push rods between the pilot's controls and the control surface, electric cables are used. Four cables are fitted for each surface, and even if three of these fail or are shot away, the pilot can still fly the aeroplane safely.

Most fighters are designed so that the forces on the wing and tail surfaces are properly balanced at quite low speeds. The pilot uses the controls to overcome changes in the balance at high speed. On the F-16, however, the forces are balanced at high speed. At low speed, a special autopilot system is used to provide steady flight. This means that the loads at high speed are lower than they are normally and this results in smaller and lighter tail surfaces which contribute to the manoeuvrability.

Many hundreds of F-16s are being built for the US Air Force and European countries, so that for many years to come the answer to 'What 'plane was that?' will be 'An F-16'. (*above*)

DE HAVILLAND CANADA BUFFALO

The Buffalo is one of several Canadian short take-off transports. It is powered by two General Electric 3,133 shp turboprop engines, each driving a large diameter propeller, which give the aircraft an impressive performance. A distinctive feature is the flat tailplane right on top of the tailfin, the position being chosen so that the elevators are well clear of any wing turbulence created when the aircraft is flying at high angles of attack.

The main cabin can accommodate up to 41 troops, or 24 stretchers, or a variety of light guns and army vehicles. (*left*)

LOCKHEED HERCULES

The Lockheed Hercules is basically a rugged transport aircraft designed to carry up to 92 paratroops or heavy loads such as the US Army 155 mm howitzer over ranges up to 4,000 km (2,500 miles).

However, it is a very versatile aircraft and is used for many other purposes such as US Coast Guard search and rescue duties, and the recovery of satellites returning from orbit while they are descending under their parachutes.

The most famous exploit involving the Hercules was the rescue of hostages from almost certain death in a high-jack drama at Entebbe in Uganda.

BREGUET ATLANTIC

The Breguet Atlantic is a maritime patrol aircraft produced jointly by France, Belgium, the Netherlands, West Germany and the United States.

It has a 'figure-eight' fuselage, with a pressurized upper deck for the 12-man crew, seven of whom work in a central operations room, and a 9-m (30-ft) long weapons bay in the unpressurized lower portion. The accommodation, which includes a rest room and kitchen, is designed to provide comfortable conditions during patrols that can last as long as 18 hours. (*top*)

BRITISH AEROSPACE NIMROD

Based on the pioneering Comet jet-airliner, the Nimrod is the world's only long-range, jet-powered, anti-submarine and maritime patrol aircraft.

It is powered by four Rolls-Royce Spey turbofans of 5,443 kg (12,000 lb) thrust each. These allow a high speed dash to the search area to be made, but if necessary, two engines can be shut down in flight to save fuel on a long mission. With a top speed of 920 kmph (575 mph) the Nimrod is much faster than its competitors.

A vast range of electronic equipment is installed, including a long-range, air-to-surface ship radar; a MAD (magnetic anomaly detection) 'tailsting', and an electronic counter-measures pod at the top of the tail fin. The radar system can not only detect ships, but identify their type; it can also classify submarine snorts (funnels through which air is fed to the engines when the craft is submerged) and periscopes.

All kinds of anti-shipping and anti-submarine weapons can be carried in the huge 15-m (48-ft) long weapons bay, including homing torpedoes, depth charges, mines and bombs. (*centre*)

McDONNELL DOUGLAS YC-15

The YC-15 was the McDonnell Douglas entry for a US Air Force competition to find a replacement for the Lockheed Hercules. The other competitor was the YC-14, entered by Boeing.

The US Air Force requirement, to carry most of the Army's latest large, heavy guns and tanks out of small, unprepared airfields, has been met by an advanced flap system. The engines, mounted on pylons extending forward from the wing leading edge, are positioned so that the exhaust nozzles are close to the undersurfaces of the wings. This provides a high-velocity airflow which is used to 'blow' air through the two big slotted flaps, so that these provide lift at low airspeeds.

Although both the McDonnell Douglas and Boeing aircraft completed their trials relatively satisfactorily, the US Air Force has decided not to order production models of either of them at this time. However, the aircraft incorporate many new ideas which will benefit military and civilian passengers for years to come. (*lower left*)

ROCKWELL INTERNATIONAL B-1

This advanced swing-wing long-range heavy bomber was intended to replace the ageing Boeing B-52s currently forming the backbone of the US Air Force strategic bomber force.

Powered by four turbofan engines, each developing 13,608 kg (30,000 lb) thrust with afterburning, the B-1 had a maximum speed of 2,335 kmph (1,320 mph) at 15,240 m (50,000 ft) and a maximum range of 9,816 km (6,100 miles). However, it could also fly fast very low down in order to penetrate enemy radar defences. It had two bomb bays, each capable of holding up to eight special attack missiles, decoy rockets, cruise missiles or 11,340 kg (25,000 lb) of conventional bombs.

The US Air Force hoped to have 244 B-1s in order to help counter the Russian build-up of arms designed to wage aggressive war. Upon the order of President Carter, however, the project was cancelled in 1978. The four prototypes built are being used for experimental purposes. (*above*)

73

AIRLINERS

Although it is a sad fact that many 'planes since the days of the Wright *Flyer* have been used as warplanes, many aircraft have been produced for the more pleasant purposes of carrying people about for business and for pleasure.

Chief among these are undoubtedly the airliners of carrying people for business and pleasure.

Most airliners have to earn money for their owners. This means that they must be as light as possible, in order to carry the maximum number of passengers. Airliners are expected to last a long time so they must be strong as well as light.

A typical fighter or bomber may only fly a few hundred hours a year, an airliner, on the other hand, may be airborne up to ten hours every day, of every week of every month. This means that the engines, and all the components of the electrical and hydraulic systems, have to work reliably and efficiently for many thousands of hours in the air extending into periods of years. It is not easy to design a component that will do those things – and yet be light and cheap to make.

The development of the turbojet engine in the 1950s revolutionized air travel, as it did fighters and bombers. The de Havilland Comet, first of the jet airliners, flew twice as fast as its piston-engined contemporaries. Its passenger cabin was quieter and more comfortable. The jet engines enabled it to fly smoothly above the regions of stormy weather.

The Comet was followed by aircraft such as the Boeing 707 and the Douglas DC-8. In turn these have been followed by the quieter and even more comfortable 'wide-bodied' airliners such as the DC-10 and the A300 Airbus.

Pride of the world's airliners is the Concorde. This beautifully streamlined, delta-winged aircraft is busy whisking people across the Atlantic at twice the speed of sound, that is, at 2,240 kmph (1,400 mph), or faster than a rifle bullet.

The Concorde and many other airliners, are described in this section of 'What Plane Is That?'.

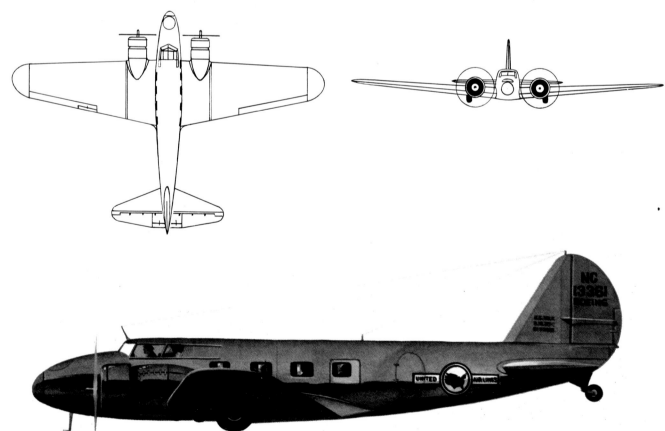

GRUMMAN GOOSE

The Goose was one of a number of small but useful amphibious aircraft built in the United States in the 1930s.

Because of its ability to operate from water as well as airfields, it was used to pioneer a number of early airline routes. It was also used extensively by the US Coast Guard service for air-sea rescue duties, flying many missions to rescue pilots or ship's crews that had got into trouble. (*top*)

BOEING 247

The Boeing 247, built in 1933, was the first 'modern' type of airliner, having an all-metal stressed skin construction, with a low-wing, two neatly-cowled air-cooled radial engines, variable-pitch propellers and a retractable undercarriage. It carried ten passengers and cruised at 248 kmph (155 mph). (*above left and left*)

BOEING 314

Built in 1938, the Boeing 314 was a large majestic trans-oceanic flying-boat which proved to be a success on both Pacific and Atlantic routes. The 314 could be readily identified by its three fins and by the distinctive wing-like hydro-stabilisers on each side of the hull just above the water-line. The four 1600 hp Wright Cyclone radial engines were accessible in flight through a companion-way inside the wing.

Up to 77 passengers, together with 11 crew members, could be carried in the double-decked hull, while mail and cargo compartments could hold nearly 5 tons of freight. At an all-up weight of 38,101 kg (84,000 lb) the normal range was 5,930 km (3,685 miles), with a normal cruising speed of 301 kmph (188 mph) at 3,748 m (11,000 ft).

British Overseas Airways Corporation obtained three 314s in 1941, when Europe was at war and Britain was virtually isolated from her friends and allies. (*above*)

FORD TRIMOTOR

Many aircraft, for one reason or another, are given a nick-name which bears little or no resemblance to the name allocated by the manufacturer. The Ford Trimotor was one such 'plane, when early in its career in the mid-1920s it was dubbed the 'Tin Goose' because of the corrugated metal skin construction.

On 28 November 1929, a place was reserved in aviation history when the first flight over the South Pole was accomplished by a Trimotor under the command of Commander R. E. Byrd of the US Navy.

A number of Trimotors are still flying in America for joy-riding purposes. However, be careful if you think that 'that 'plane was a Trimotor', as it could be the very similar Bushmaster 2000, built in 1966.

VICKERS VISCOUNT

The propeller turbine engine, perhaps better known as the turboprop engine, or in America as the propjet, was pioneered in Britain. A gas turbine engine drives a propeller through reduction gears, and with the added benefit of thrust from the jet exhaust, the turboprop engine has all the smoothness of a pure turbojet engine, but it costs less to operate.

The first civilian transport aircraft in the world to be powered by turboprop engines was the Viscount, which first flew in 1948, using four Rolls-Royce Dart engines.

Development of a more powerful Dart engine soon enabled an enlarged version of the Viscount to be produced, capable of carrying between 47 and 60 passengers. In this form the Viscount became a success with airlines and passengers all over the world, and it has the distinction of being the first ever British airliner to enter regular service with an American airline.

In terms of world-wide sales, the Viscount has proved to be Britain's most successful large airliner. (*above and top right*)

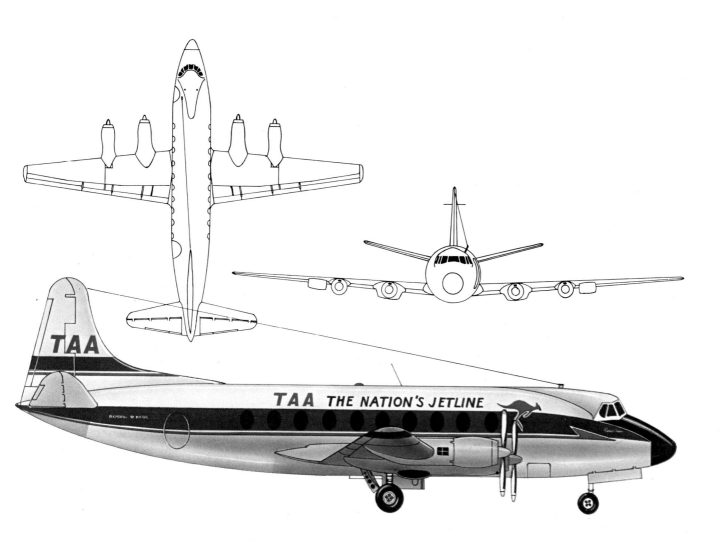

LOCKHEED ELECTRA

This was the only large civilian propjet airliner to be produced in America. Capable of carrying up to 99 passengers, the Lockheed L.188 Electra first flew in 1957 and was powered by four 3,750 hp Allison engines.

Designed specifically as a medium-range airliner for routes in America, nearly 200 of these aircraft were produced. Entering service in 1959, with various airlines in America, and with KLM Royal Dutch Airlines in Europe, the Electra served usefully in the interim period before the development of turbojet airliners. (*left*)

LOCKHEED SUPER CONSTELLATION

In 1939 the Lockheed Aircraft Corporation was working on the prototype of an intercontinental airliner, designated L-49, later to be named Constellation. Before the prototype could be completed however, America entered World War II and the 'plane was changed into a military transport, the C-69. After the war, Lockheed produced a pressurized-cabin version of the Constellation, designated L-049 and it was from this that the L-1049 Super Constellation was developed.

In 1953 the L-1049C was introduced, fitted with four of the new Wright Turbo-Cyclone compound piston engines which gave some 20% increase in range for the same fuel consumption.

Shown in the photograph is a L-1049G Super Constellation, which has wing tip fuel tanks which increased the range. (*left*)

BOEING 707

The first American jet transport aircraft to fly was the Boeing 367-80. This aircraft, developed initially as a military in-flight refuelling tanker, was the prototype for the 707 and the famous family of airliners which followed, which have made the Boeing Company the leading commercial aircraft manufacturer in the world. This first 707 was an advanced aircraft with swept-wings and four pod-mounted engines, and it embodied all the experience gained during the development of previous military jet aircraft. A new era in civil air transport began with the introduction of this aircraft.

Apart from seeing service with the major airlines of the world, versions of the 707 are produced for military duties such as anti-submarine warfare (ASW), long-range patrol, in-flight tanker refuelling, and Airborne Warning and Control Systems (AWACS). There are also VIP versions which are made to special order, similar to the one used by the President of the United States.

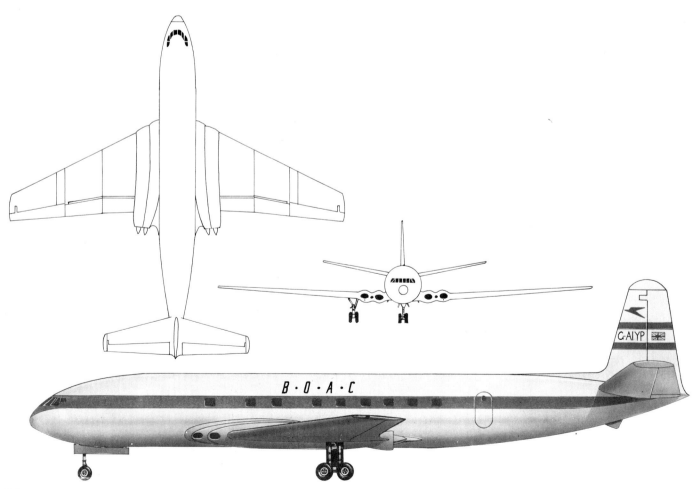

DE HAVILLAND COMET

The Comet was the world's first pure-jet airliner to fly (1949) and to enter airline service (1952). For a year or so it appeared that Britain had a real winner in the Comet, with its high speed, smooth flight, regular operations and undeniably beautiful lines. Sadly, however, tragedy struck and three of them were lost in a series of fatal and mysterious crashes. The Comet was withdrawn from service and intensive investigations revealed the cause to be metal fatigue which allowed the pressurized cabin to burst apart. There can be little doubt, however, that the lessons learned made future airliners all over the world, much safer for passengers.

The Comet 4 was introduced as a redesigned version, and in 1958 British Overseas Airways Corporation used one of these to operate the first-ever transatlantic jet airliner service.

In 1960 a shorter-span and longer-fuselage version, the Comet 4B, was introduced for use by British European Airways. Today, a military development known as the Nimrod is being used for anti-submarine and reconnaissance duties. (*above left and left*)

CONVAIR CV-880

Designed for use by American domestic airlines, this was a swept-wing airliner with a capacity for up to 130 passengers. Powered by four General Electric turbojet engines, it could cruise at up to 989 kmph (615 mph) but it was considerably smaller than its more successful counterparts of the day, the Boeing 707 and the Douglas DC-8. Only 65 of the airliners were built. (*top*)

DOUGLAS DC-8

This aircraft, the first jet airliner to be manufactured by the Douglas Aircraft Co., was produced in several versions all of which were very successful. The differing versions included freight, convertible, mixed passenger/cargo, and long-range types. Largest of the DC-8s was the -63 which was introduced by KLM (Royal Dutch Airlines) on the Amsterdam to New York route in 1967, with a seating capacity for up to 269 passengers and a maximum weight of 158,756 kg (350,000 lb). (*above*)

85

TUPOLEV Tu-134

The Tu-134 is a twin-turbofan airliner designed to carry up to 72 passengers over ranges of up to 2,400 km (1,500 miles). It is built by the factory which produced Russia's first jet airliner, the Tu-104, and the world's first supersonic airliner, the Tu-144.

Shown in the photograph are the markings of Russia's Aeroflot, the world's biggest airline. The Tu-134 is also in service with a number of Eastern European countries.

The Tu-134 has been given the NATO reporting code name of 'Crusty'. (*above*)

HAWKER SIDDELEY TRIDENT 3B

The Trident 3B was the last major version of the Trident series of aircraft, which were originally designed for British European Airways (BEA) as short-to-medium-range airliners.

The Trident is a low-wing monoplane with high T-tail and three rear-mounted Rolls-Royce Spey turbofan engines. In addition, all 3B versions have a tail-mounted Rolls-Royce 162 booster engine to improve take-off performance.

The final variant of the type was the Super Trident 3B, with a maximum weight of 73,935 kg (163,000 lb), a range of 3,379 km (2,100 miles) and seating for 152 passengers.

Tridents have played a major part in the development of automatic landing, the very first automatic landing by an aircraft in passenger service being accomplished in 1965 by a Trident arriving at London's Heathrow from Paris. (*left*)

BOEING 747SP

The Boeing 747 is the world's biggest airliner, with a main passenger cabin 56.99 m (187 ft) long by 6.81 m (20 ft) wide and having a cabin ceiling height of 3.6 m (8 ft). The flight deck is on an upper level and behind this is a smaller cabin which is usually reserved for first-class passengers, or arranged as a lounge and bar area. The 747 fully deserves its popular but unofficial nickname 'Jumbojet'.

In 1975 Boeing introduced the SP (Special Performance) version, with a fuselage length of 55 m (181 ft), some 15 m (50 ft) shorter than the standard 747, and with a fin which was 2.26 m (5 ft) taller. This distinctive variation was designed for very long-range operations on routes where there was a requirement for a smaller-capacity 747.

With a full load of 321 passengers, including 32 in the upper cabin, the SP version can fly 11,106 km (6,900 miles) non-stop. On a delivery flight in 1976, a 747SP of South African Airways flew non-stop from Seattle to Cape Town, a distance of 13,382 km (10,290 miles), in 17 hours 22 minutes. (*above*)

DASSAULT MYSTÈRE FALCON 20

The French-produced Falcon normally carries a crew of two and up to ten passengers but this can be increased to fourteen by removing the tables inside. It was the first business jet to be powered by turbofan jet engines which are now commonly used in modern business jets.

BOEING 727

The Boeing 727 is the most successful airliner in the world, with sales exceeding 1,500. No other airliner has exceeded a sales figure of one thousand.

Carrying up to 189 passengers, the 727 is designed for short-to-medium ranges to complement the long-range Boeing 707. Compared with the 707, a major change was the decision to mount all three engines at the rear of the fuselage, a layout previously adopted by de Havilland for the Trident and since by Russian designers.

The latest 727s, known as 727-200s, have improved cabins compared with early versions, giving a more spacious appearance, and many improvements embodied in the various systems. Some aircraft have what is called Automatic Power Reserve installed. APR senses any significant loss in thrust by an engine during take-off and initial climb, and automatically increases the thrust on the other two engines from 7,439 kg (16,400 lb) to 7,892 kg (17,400 lb). This feature improves the performance of the 727 when operating from 'hot and high' airfields, that is, from airports where the density of the air (and hence the thrust of the engines) is lower than normal. (*top*)

BOEING 737

Smallest of the Boeing family of jet airliners, the 737 is a short-range airliner carrying up to 130 passengers over ranges of around 3,200 km (2,000 miles).

In addition to the many hundreds which are in airline service, a number of 737s are being used as business jets. These can carry up to 15 passengers in exceptionally comfortable and luxurious cabins. (*left*)

AIRBUS INDUSTRIE A-300

The A300 is a 220–320 seat wide-body airliner, designed and built in Europe, and powered by American General Electric engines. It is in service with many airlines all over the world, including Eastern Airlines in the United States.

Two basic versions of the A300 are manufactured, the B2 and the B4; both are the same size, but the B4 has a longer range, due to a larger fuel capacity.

Both versions are normally powered by two wing-mounted General Electric CF6-50 turbofan engines, each of which develops 51,000 pounds of thrust. The A300 is the quietest wide-body aircraft in service, so if you should spot one but can hardly hear it, you may be tempted to say 'What a quiet 'plane that was'. (*top left*)

McDONNELL DOUGLAS DC-10

Designed to meet the specialized requirements of American Airlines, the DC-10 is a wide-bodied airliner seating up to 380 passengers. American Airlines appreciated that increasing airport congestion would be alleviated by the introduction of airliners of greater passenger-carrying capacity, but also considered it important that such aircraft should not be restricted to airports having very long runways.

In the early project design stage, the DC-10 was a twin-engined aircraft, but as the design evolved the major decision was made to use three engines. Two of the engines are mounted conventionally under the wing, but the third engine is mounted, very distinctively, in the base of the fin, above the fuselage. On other tri-jets such as the Hawker Siddeley Trident and Lockheed L-1011 TriStar, the third engines are installed inside the tail of the fuselage, fed by air intake in front of the fin. (*bottom left*)

LOCKHEED L-1011 TRISTAR

When it was first introduced in 1970, the Tri-Star was the first aircraft to be powered by the advanced technology RB.211 turbofan engines developed by Rolls-Royce.

The seating capacity of the TriStar can be varied to suit 272 passengers in a mixed-class layout or up to 400 passengers in an economy-class layout. Externally the TriStar is very similar in appearance to the Douglas DC-10, which also has two wing-mounted engines and one tail-mounted engine. To identify which aircraft is which, remember that the TriStar has the rear engine mounted inside the fuselage, with the air intake above the fuselage forward of the fin, whereas the DC-10 has its rear engine mounted in the fin. Both of these aircraft are in the 'wide-body' airliner category, a term first given to describe the Boeing 747 jumbojet. (*above*)

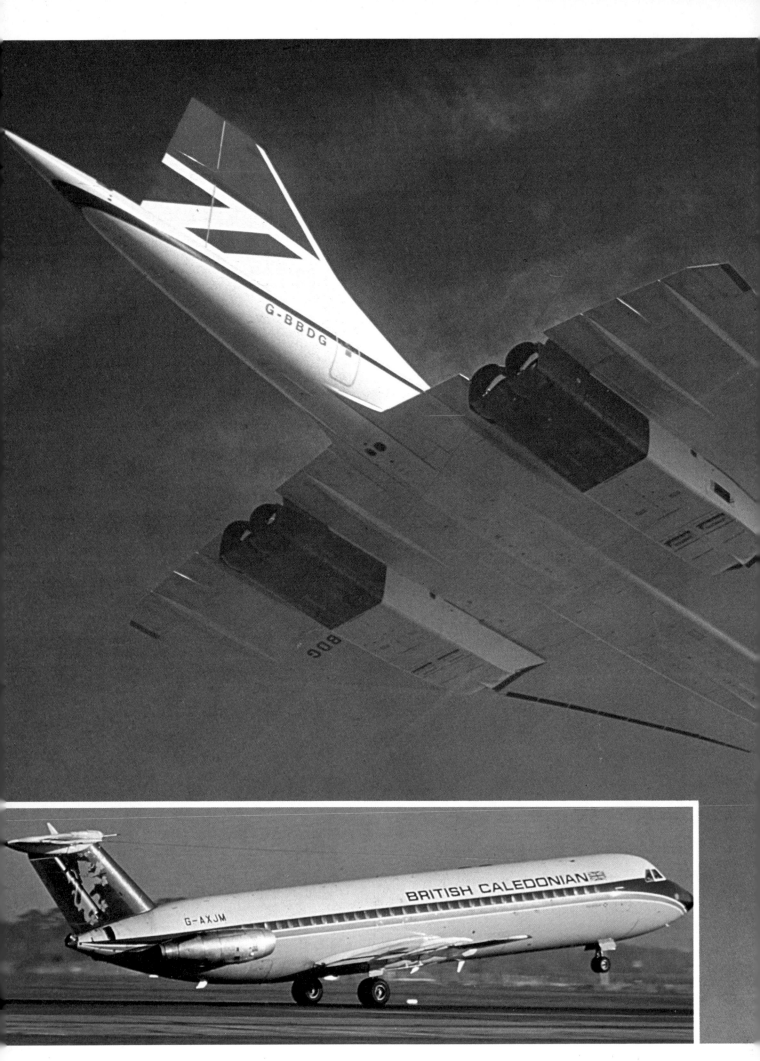

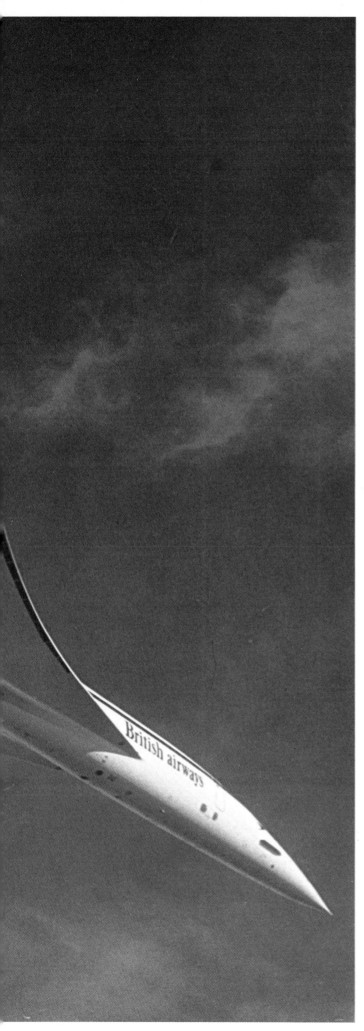

AEROSPATIALE/BAC CONCORDE

Concorde is a delta-winged, supersonic transport, capable of cruising at over Mach 2, about 2,245 kmph (1,400 mph), carrying 128 passengers at a height of 18,288 km (60,000 ft). It is powered by four Olympus 593 turbojet engines which, with reheat, each develop over 17,236 kg (38,000 lb) thrust.

This aircraft is the product of international collaboration between Britain and France. From its conception, some 20 years ago, Concorde has been the centre of controversy. On the one hand there are those critics who declare that the aircraft is a burden on the British and French taxpayer, and a noisy monster which will pollute the atmosphere. On the other hand are those that applaud a great technical achievement and regard Concorde for what it is, a masterpiece of aeronautical engineering that heralds the dawn of a new era of swift transportation.

The basically simple exterior of Concorde hides the complexity of the internal systems and equipment. For example, the fuel system is also used to maintain aircraft trim and to cool the cabin air. After take-off and climb, reheat is selected to enable the aircraft to pass quickly through the region of transonic drag rise. To compensate for the change in the centre of pressure during this period, fuel is transferred from tanks in the front of the wing to tanks in the rear. The centre of gravity is therefore shifted with the centre of pressure, and aircraft trim is maintained without the need for changes in settings of flying controls, in this case the elevons, which would increase the drag.

Although the TU-144, which in general shape resembles Concorde, was the first supersonic transport to fly (some 3 months before Concorde) it has not been very successful in spite of extensive design changes, while Concorde is in regular passenger service with British Airways and Air France.

The photograph shows Concorde in British Airways colours, taking off with reheat applied. For take-off the nose is drooped and the visor fully retracted. (*left*)

BRITISH AEROSPACE 1-11

Before a new aircraft is 'launched' a great deal of research is done into what kind of aircraft the world's airlines require. Such was the case of the One-Eleven, which was the first of its type to be designed to meet the requirement for a smaller twin-jet aircraft than the Boeing 707 'family', Douglas DC-8, Convair 880 and the Hawker Siddeley Trident.

Several versions of the One Eleven have been produced and the airliner is used by a large number of airlines all over the world.

Shown in the photograph is a Series 500, operated by British Caledonian, with seating for up to 109 passengers. (*far left*)

INDEX

ACKNOWLEDGEMENTS

The publishers would like to thank the following organisations and individuals for their kind permission to reproduce the photographs in this book:

Air Portraits: 36ab, 45; Basil Arkell: 22ab & centre; Associated Press: 61bel; Bell Helicopter Company: 24; The Boeing Company: 32–3, 40–1, 42–3, 76, 82–3, 90–1; British Aircraft Corporation: 94bel; Dassault-Breguet Aviation: 50bel, 54ab, 72ab; General Dynamics Corporation: 68–9; James Gilbert: 16 centre & bel, 18bel; Hawker Siddeley Aviation: 56–7, 86; Leslie Hunt: 34, 36bel, 38ab & centre; Howard Levy: 26, 27, 64; Lockheed Aircraft Corporation: 70–1, 80bel, 93–5; Ministry of Defence: 48bel, 52–3, 62–3, 72 centre; David Mondey: 54–5; John Moore: 48ab; Photri: 68bel; John Rigby: 36 centre, 66–7, 88–9, 92ab; Herbert Rittmeyer: 30ab, 37ab; Rockwell International Corporation: 73; Saab-Scania Aktiebolag: 68ab; Spectrum: 1, 4–5, 6–7, 14–15, 74–5, (G. R. Tearle) endpapers; Tony Stone Associates: 17bel; J. Stroud: 80ab, 87bel; M. Taylor: 8–12, 16ab, 17ab, 18ab, 19, 22bel, 23bel, 25, 26–7, 28–9, 30bel, 31, 35, 37bel, 38bel, 40 inset, 41, 44, 44–5, 46, 47ab, 48 centre, 49, 50ab & centre, 51, 53 inset, 54bel, 58–60, 61ab, 63 inset, 64–5, 70 inset, 72bel, 77–9, 81, 84–5, 87ab, 92bel; Westland Helicopters Limited: 23ab; Gordon Williams: 47bel; Zefa: 20–1, (Gradl) 2–3.